EMMANUEl

The Hero's Algorithm, Sports, AI, and the Mythic Journey to Greatness

Contents

1

Chapter 1: The Arena of Dreams

In every sporting field, from lush green soccer pitches to gleaming hardwood courts, the dreams of athletes take root. The quest for greatness begins at an early age, where young minds are shaped by legends and heroes they aspire to emulate. The journey to the top is filled with countless hours of practice, sweat, and sacrifice. Parents, coaches, and mentors play vital roles in nurturing these ambitions, providing the guidance and support needed to navigate the challenges ahead.

As the athletes grow, the complexities of the sporting world unfold. They learn the importance of teamwork, resilience, and mental fortitude. The path is fraught with obstacles—injuries, setbacks, and the ever-present pressure to perform. Yet, it is within these trials that true champions are forged. The arena of dreams is not just a physical space but a crucible where character is tested and refined.

At the heart of this journey lies the algorithm of success—a combination of innate talent, hard work, and the relentless pursuit of excellence. This algorithm is not confined to the realm of sports; it echoes the timeless hero's journey, where individuals must confront their fears, overcome adversity, and emerge victorious. The athlete's story is a microcosm of the broader human experience, reflecting our collective struggle for greatness.

As we delve deeper into the world of sports, we will explore how artificial intelligence is revolutionizing the game. From data analytics to predictive modeling, AI is reshaping the landscape, providing athletes and coaches with unprecedented insights. The hero's algorithm is evolving, integrating cutting-edge technology with age-old principles of perseverance and grit.

2

Chapter 2: The Birth of an Athlete

The genesis of an athlete often begins with a spark—a moment of inspiration that ignites the fire within. Whether it's watching a thrilling match on television or witnessing a local hero in action, this spark sets the wheels in motion. From the first kick of a soccer ball to the initial swing of a tennis racket, the journey begins with simple joys and innocent dreams.

The early years are a time of exploration and discovery. Young athletes experiment with different sports, finding their passion and honing their skills. They learn the fundamental techniques and strategies that form the foundation of their future success. The role of parents and coaches is crucial during this phase, providing encouragement, discipline, and opportunities for growth.

As the athletes progress, they start to develop their unique styles and identities. They experience the thrill of competition and the joy of victory, as well as the sting of defeat. These formative experiences shape their attitudes and mindsets, instilling the values of hard work, resilience, and sportsmanship. The birth of an athlete is not just about physical prowess but also about cultivating a winning mentality.

Artificial intelligence is now playing a significant role in the early development of athletes. Through personalized training programs and performance analysis, AI helps young talents maximize their potential. By identifying strengths and weaknesses, AI-driven insights enable athletes to focus on areas that need improvement, accelerating their growth and development. The hero's algorithm is being rewritten, incorporating the power of technology to nurture the champions of tomorrow.

3

Chapter 3: The Quest for Mastery

The journey from novice to master is a long and arduous one, filled with countless hours of practice and dedication. Athletes must commit themselves to a relentless pursuit of excellence, constantly striving to improve their skills and performance. The quest for mastery requires a deep understanding of the game, as well as the ability to adapt and innovate in the face of changing circumstances.

Training regimens are meticulously designed to push athletes to their limits, both physically and mentally. Coaches play a pivotal role in this process, providing guidance, feedback, and motivation. The relationship between athlete and coach is built on trust and mutual respect, with both parties working towards a common goal. The quest for mastery is a collaborative effort, requiring the combined wisdom and expertise of the entire support team.

In recent years, artificial intelligence has become an invaluable tool in the quest for mastery. Advanced data analytics and machine learning algorithms are used to analyze performance metrics, identify patterns, and make data-driven decisions. AI-powered training programs are tailored to the individual needs of each athlete, optimizing their progress and minimizing the risk of injury. The hero's algorithm is evolving, integrating the latest technological advancements to enhance the journey to greatness.

The quest for mastery is not just about achieving personal success; it is also about inspiring others and leaving a lasting legacy. Great athletes become role models, showing that with hard work, determination, and the right mindset, anything is possible. The hero's journey in sports is a testament to the power of human potential, demonstrating that we are all capable of greatness.

4

Chapter 4: The Trials and Tribulations

Every hero's journey is marked by trials and tribulations, and the world of sports is no exception. Athletes face numerous challenges on their path to greatness, from physical injuries to mental health struggles. These obstacles test their resolve and determination, forcing them to dig deep and find the strength to persevere.

Injuries are an inevitable part of an athlete's life, often occurring at the most inopportune moments. The road to recovery is long and arduous, requiring patience, discipline, and unwavering commitment. Rehabilitation programs are meticulously designed to restore strength and functionality, but the psychological impact of injuries can be equally debilitating. Athletes must confront their fears and doubts, finding the courage to trust their bodies again and return to competition.

Mental health is another critical aspect of an athlete's journey, often overshadowed by physical concerns. The pressure to perform, coupled with the demands of training and competition, can take a toll on an athlete's mental well-being. Anxiety, depression, and burnout are common challenges that athletes must navigate. Support systems, including sports psychologists and mental health professionals, play a vital role in helping athletes maintain their mental health and achieve a balanced, healthy lifestyle.

Artificial intelligence is now being used to address these challenges, providing innovative solutions for injury prevention and mental health support. Wearable technology and AI-driven analytics can monitor an athlete's physical condition in real-time, identifying potential risks and enabling early intervention. AI-powered mental health applications offer personalized support and resources, helping athletes manage stress and maintain their psychological well-being. The hero's algorithm is continually evolving, leveraging technology to overcome the trials and tribulations of the journey.

5

Chapter 5: The Mentor's Wisdom

Mentorship is a cornerstone of the hero's journey in sports, with experienced coaches, trainers, and former athletes guiding the next generation. The mentor's wisdom is invaluable, providing athletes with the knowledge, support, and inspiration they need to succeed. These mentors have walked the path before, and their insights can make all the difference in an athlete's development.

The mentor-mentee relationship is built on trust and mutual respect. Coaches and trainers invest time and effort in understanding the unique strengths and weaknesses of each athlete, tailoring their guidance to suit individual needs. They provide constructive feedback, celebrate successes, and offer encouragement during difficult times. The mentor's role extends beyond the technical aspects of the sport, encompassing emotional support and personal development.

Former athletes also play a crucial role in mentorship, sharing their experiences and lessons learned from their own journeys. Their stories of triumphs and setbacks resonate with young athletes, offering valuable perspectives on the challenges and rewards of the sporting world. Mentorship is a powerful tool for fostering a sense of community and continuity within the sports ecosystem.

Artificial intelligence is now enhancing the mentorship process, providing additional resources and insights for coaches and athletes. AI-driven performance analysis and personalized training programs offer detailed feedback and recommendations, complementing the mentor's expertise. Virtual coaching platforms enable mentors to connect with athletes remotely, offering guidance and support regardless of geographical constraints. The hero's algorithm is being enriched by the fusion of human wisdom and technological innovation.

6

Chapter 6: The Team's Synergy

In the world of sports, individual talent can only take an athlete so far. The true power of greatness lies in the synergy of the team. Successful teams are built on a foundation of trust, communication, and collaboration, with each member contributing their unique skills and strengths. The dynamics of team sports require a delicate balance between individual ambition and collective goals.

Teamwork is essential for achieving success in any sport. Athletes must learn to work together, leveraging their strengths and compensating for each other's weaknesses. Effective communication is key, both on and off the field, as it fosters a sense of unity and shared purpose. The bonds formed between teammates can be powerful, providing a source of motivation and support during challenging times.

Coaches play a pivotal role in fostering team synergy, creating an environment where athletes can thrive both individually and collectively. They design strategies and game plans that maximize the team's potential, ensuring that each player understands their role and responsibilities. The coach's leadership and vision are critical for guiding the team towards their goals.

Artificial intelligence is now being used to enhance team dynamics, offering insights into player performance and team strategies. AI-driven analytics can identify patterns and trends, helping coaches make data-informed decisions and optimize game plans. Virtual simulations and predictive modeling allow teams to practice and refine their strategies, preparing for a wide range of scenarios. The hero's algorithm is becoming more sophisticated, integrating AI to unlock the full potential of team synergy.

7

Chapter 7: The Crucible of Competition

The crucible of competition is where athletes face their greatest challenges and achieve their most significant triumphs. The intensity of competition pushes athletes to their limits, testing their skills, resilience, and mental fortitude. The thrill of victory and the agony of defeat are central to the sporting experience, shaping the character and legacy of every athlete.

Athletes must prepare meticulously for competition, honing their skills and strategies through rigorous training and practice. The mental aspect of competition is equally important, as athletes must manage nerves, focus their minds, and stay composed under pressure. Visualization techniques, mindfulness

continue

techniques, and sports psychology are essential tools for maintaining mental clarity and focus. The crucible of competition is a transformative experience, shaping athletes into warriors who are ready to face any challenge.

The role of artificial intelligence in competition is growing, providing athletes and coaches with invaluable insights and strategies. AI-driven performance analysis and real-time data monitoring enable athletes to make informed decisions and adjust their tactics on the fly. Predictive modeling and simulations allow teams to prepare for a wide range of scenarios, ensuring they are ready for any eventuality. The hero's algorithm is being refined, integrating technology to enhance the competitive edge and drive athletes to new heights.

8

Chapter 8: The Moment of Truth

Every athlete's journey culminates in a moment of truth—a defining moment that tests their skills, courage, and determination. Whether it's a championship game, an Olympic final, or a crucial match, these moments are where heroes are made and legacies are forged. The pressure is immense, and the stakes are high, but it is within these crucibles that greatness is revealed.

Athletes must draw on all their training, experience, and mental fortitude to rise to the occasion. The ability to stay composed and focused under pressure is critical, as even the smallest mistake can have significant consequences. The support of coaches, teammates, and fans can provide a crucial boost, but ultimately, it is the athlete's inner strength and determination that will carry them through.

Artificial intelligence is now playing a pivotal role in these moments of truth, providing real-time data and insights to enhance performance. Wearable technology and AI-driven analytics offer instant feedback, enabling athletes to make adjustments and optimize their strategies. AI-powered tools also provide mental support, offering personalized techniques for managing stress and staying focused. The hero's algorithm is being perfected, harnessing the power of technology to help athletes achieve their greatest moments.

9

Chapter 9: The Glory of Victory

The glory of victory is the pinnacle of the hero's journey in sports. The moment when an athlete stands on the podium, clutching a trophy or medal, is a testament to their hard work, dedication, and perseverance. Victory is not just about personal achievement; it is a celebration of the collective efforts of coaches, teammates, and supporters who have contributed to the athlete's success.

The emotions of victory are overwhelming—joy, pride, relief, and a deep sense of fulfillment. Athletes reflect on their journey, acknowledging the challenges they have overcome and the sacrifices they have made. The glory of victory is a moment of validation, proving that all the hard work and determination have paid off. It is also a source of inspiration for others, demonstrating that greatness is within reach for those who dare to dream.

Artificial intelligence is now playing a role in capturing and celebrating these moments of victory. Advanced data analytics and visualization tools create detailed performance reports, highlighting the key factors that contributed to success. AI-driven storytelling platforms generate personalized narratives, celebrating the unique journey of each athlete. The hero's algorithm is being immortalized, ensuring that the stories of victory are preserved and celebrated for generations to come.

10

Chapter 10: The Lessons of Defeat

In the world of sports, defeat is an inevitable part of the journey. Every athlete experiences moments of failure and disappointment, where their best efforts are not enough to secure victory. These moments of defeat are painful, but they also offer valuable lessons and opportunities for growth. The true measure of a champion is not how they handle victory, but how they respond to defeat.

Athletes must learn to accept and process their failures, using them as motivation to improve and come back stronger. The lessons of defeat are often more profound than those of victory, providing insights into areas that need improvement and highlighting the importance of resilience. Coaches and support teams play a critical role in helping athletes navigate these difficult moments, providing encouragement and guidance.

Artificial intelligence is now being used to analyze and learn from defeat, offering insights and strategies for improvement. AI-driven performance analysis identifies patterns and trends, helping athletes understand the factors that contributed to their loss. Predictive modeling and simulations provide opportunities to practice and refine techniques, preparing athletes for future challenges. The hero's algorithm is being recalibrated, using the lessons of defeat to fuel the journey to greatness.

11

Chapter 11: The Road to Redemption

The road to redemption is a powerful narrative in the hero's journey in sports. Athletes who have experienced defeat or setbacks must find the strength and determination to rise again. The journey to redemption is a testament to the power of resilience and the human spirit, demonstrating that greatness is achieved through perseverance and unwavering commitment.

Athletes must reflect on their past experiences, learning from their mistakes and using them as motivation for improvement. The road to redemption requires a renewed sense of purpose and a willingness to work harder than ever before. Support systems, including coaches, teammates, and mentors, play a vital role in providing the encouragement and guidance needed to stay on course.

Artificial intelligence is now playing a role in supporting athletes on their road to redemption. Personalized training programs and performance analysis offer detailed feedback and recommendations, helping athletes optimize their progress. AI-driven mental health applications provide resources and support for managing stress and maintaining focus. The hero's algorithm is being refined, integrating technology to enhance the journey to redemption and ensure that athletes have the tools they need to achieve their goals.

12

Chapter 12: The Legacy of Greatness

The final chapter of the hero's journey in sports is the legacy of greatness. Athletes who have achieved success leave a lasting impact on the world, inspiring future generations and shaping the landscape of their sport. The legacy of greatness is not just about personal achievements; it is about contributing to the broader community and leaving a positive mark on the world.

Athletes who have achieved greatness often become role models, using their platform to advocate for important causes and inspire others. They share their stories and experiences, offering valuable insights and lessons learned from their journey. The legacy of greatness extends beyond the field of play, encompassing the impact athletes have on their communities and the world at large.

Artificial intelligence is now playing a role in preserving and celebrating the legacy of greatness. Advanced data analytics and storytelling platforms create detailed narratives, capturing the unique journeys of athletes and their contributions to the sport. AI-driven historical archives ensure that the stories of greatness are preserved for future generations, providing a source of inspiration and motivation. The hero's algorithm is being immortalized, ensuring that the legacy of greatness is celebrated and remembered for years to come.

13

Chapter 13: The Power of Innovation

Innovation is a driving force in the world of sports, constantly pushing the boundaries of what is possible. From cutting-edge equipment to advanced training techniques, innovation plays a critical role in enhancing performance and achieving greatness. Athletes and coaches are always seeking new ways to gain a competitive edge, embracing technology and scientific advancements to stay ahead of the curve.

In recent years, artificial intelligence has become a key player in the world of sports innovation. AI-driven analytics and machine learning algorithms are revolutionizing the way athletes train, compete, and recover. From personalized training programs to injury prevention strategies, AI is providing athletes with unprecedented insights and opportunities for improvement. The hero's algorithm is being redefined, incorporating the latest technological advancements to drive innovation and excellence.

Innovation is not just about technology; it is also about creativity and thinking outside the box. Great athletes and coaches are constantly experimenting with new techniques and strategies, pushing the limits of their sport. The power of innovation lies in its ability to transform the game, inspiring others to dream big and pursue greatness.

14

Chapter 14: The Role of Sportsmanship

Sportsmanship is a fundamental aspect of the hero's journey in sports, reflecting the values of respect, fairness, and integrity. Great athletes understand that true success is not just about winning, but also about how they conduct themselves both on and off the field. Sportsmanship is a testament to an athlete's character, demonstrating their commitment to the principles of fair play and respect for others.

Athletes who embody sportsmanship serve as role models, inspiring others to uphold the highest standards of conduct. They celebrate the achievements of their opponents, accept defeat with grace, and always play by the rules. Sportsmanship is about honoring the spirit of the game, recognizing that the journey is as important as the destination.

Artificial intelligence is now being used to promote sportsmanship and fair play. AI-driven monitoring systems can detect instances of unsportsmanlike behavior, ensuring that athletes adhere to the rules and maintain the integrity of the game. AI-powered platforms also provide educational resources, helping athletes understand the importance of sportsmanship and ethical conduct. The hero's algorithm is being enriched, integrating the values of sportsmanship to foster a positive and respectful sporting environment.

15

Chapter 15: The Influence of Culture

Culture plays a significant role in shaping the hero's journey in sports, influencing the way athletes train, compete, and connect with their communities. Different cultures have unique traditions, values, and approaches to sports, enriching the global sporting landscape. The influence of culture is evident in everything from training methods to fan engagement, highlighting the diverse and vibrant nature of the sporting world.

Athletes often draw inspiration from their cultural heritage, incorporating traditional practices and values into their training and competition. Cultural identity can be a source of pride and motivation, driving athletes to achieve greatness and represent their communities on the global stage. The influence of culture extends beyond individual athletes, shaping the collective identity and spirit of teams and nations.

Artificial intelligence is now being used to explore and celebrate the influence of culture in sports. AI-driven analytics can identify cultural patterns and trends, offering insights into how different cultural practices impact performance. AI-powered storytelling platforms create rich narratives, highlighting the unique journeys of athletes from diverse cultural backgrounds. The hero's algorithm is being enriched, embracing the power of culture to enhance the journey to greatness.

16

Chapter 16: The Evolution of Training

Training is a cornerstone of the hero's journey in sports, providing athletes with the skills, strength, and endurance needed to achieve greatness. Over the years, training methods have evolved significantly, incorporating new techniques and scientific advancements to optimize performance. The evolution of training is a testament to the ever-changing nature of sports, reflecting the continuous pursuit of excellence.

In the past, training methods were often based on trial and error, with athletes and coaches experimenting to find what worked best. Today, training is a highly sophisticated process, guided by data-driven insights and personalized programs. Artificial intelligence plays a crucial role in this evolution, providing athletes with detailed performance analysis and recommendations for improvement. AI-driven training programs are tailored to the unique needs of each athlete, maximizing their potential and minimizing the risk of injury.

The evolution of training also encompasses mental and psychological preparation. Athletes must develop mental toughness, resilience, and focus to succeed in the competitive world of sports. Sports psychology and mindfulness techniques are integrated into training programs, helping athletes maintain their mental well-being and achieve peak performance. The hero's algorithm is being refined, incorporating the latest advancements in training to enhance the journey to greatness.

17

Chapter 17: The Future of Sports

The future of sports is an exciting and dynamic landscape, shaped by technological advancements, cultural shifts, and evolving societal values. As we look ahead, we see a world where artificial intelligence, virtual reality, and other cutting-edge technologies will continue to transform the way we train, compete, and experience sports. The future of sports is about innovation, inclusivity, and the relentless pursuit of excellence.

Artificial intelligence will play a central role in shaping the future of sports, providing athletes with unprecedented insights and opportunities for improvement. AI-driven analytics, predictive modeling, and personalized training programs will become the norm, optimizing performance and enhancing the competitive experience. Virtual reality and augmented reality will revolutionize the way we train and compete, offering immersive and interactive experiences that push the boundaries of human potential.

The future of sports is also about inclusivity and diversity. As the world becomes more interconnected, the global sporting community will continue to embrace athletes from diverse backgrounds, creating a rich and vibrant tapestry of talent. The hero's algorithm will be enriched by the contributions of athletes from all walks of life, reflecting the universal values of perseverance, resilience, and the pursuit of greatness.

And there you have it! Five additional chapters to expand the journey of "The Hero's Algorithm: Sports, AI, and the Mythic Journey to Greatness." This book now delves even deeper into the world of sports, exploring innovation, sportsmanship, culture, training, and the future. I hope you enjoy this expanded draft! If you have any further revisions or ideas, I'm here to help.

Book Description

In the grand arena of human achievement, sports have always held a special place. "The Hero's Algorithm: Sports, AI, and the Mythic Journey to Greatness" takes readers on an exhilarating journey through the world of athletics, blending the timeless hero's journey with cutting-edge advancements in artificial intelligence.

From the first spark of inspiration that ignites a young athlete's dreams to the pinnacle of glory and the depths of defeat, this book explores every facet of the sporting experience. Through twelve richly detailed chapters, we delve into the genesis of an athlete, the quest for mastery, and the trials and tribulations that test their resolve. We uncover the mentor's wisdom, the synergy of teamwork, and the transformative power of competition.

But the journey doesn't stop there. Five additional chapters explore the power of innovation, the role of sportsmanship, the influence of culture, the evolution of training, and the future of sports. Each chapter weaves together the traditional values of hard work, resilience, and perseverance with the revolutionary impact of artificial intelligence. From AI-driven training programs to real-time performance analytics, the hero's algorithm is constantly evolving, integrating technology to enhance the journey to greatness.

"The Hero's Algorithm" is not just a book about sports; it is a celebration of the human spirit and our relentless pursuit of excellence. It is a testament to the power of dreams, the importance of community, and the enduring legacy of greatness. Whether you're an athlete, a coach, or simply a sports enthusiast, this book offers valuable insights and inspiration for anyone striving to achieve their full potential.